W9-AGV-402

THE BILL OF RIGHTS

FOURTH AMENDMENT: THE RIGHT TO PRIVACY

BY RICH SMITH

SERIES CONSULTANT: SCOTT HARR, J.D. CRIMINAL JUSTICE
DEPARTMENT CHAIR, CONCORDIA UNIVERSITY ST. PAUL

VISIT US AT
WWW.ABDOPUBLISHING.COM

Published by ABDO Publishing Company, 8000 West 78th Street, Suite 310, Edina, MN 55439.
Copyright ©2008 by Abdo Consulting Group, Inc. International copyrights reserved in all countries.
No part of this book may be reproduced in any form without written permission from the publisher.
Abdo & Daughters™ is a trademark and logo of ABDO Publishing Company.

Printed in the United States.

Editor: John Hamilton
Graphic Design: John Hamilton
Cover Design: Neil Klinepier
Cover Illustration: Getty Images
Interior Photos and Illustrations: p 1 Constitution & flag, iStockphoto; p 4 security guard searches student's backpack, Getty Images; p 7 police officer seen through peephole, Corbis; p 9 federal agents search home, AP Images; p 10 FBI agents guarding door, AP Images; p 13 graffiti artist fleeing officer, Getty Images; p 15 police officer with helicopter overhead, AP Images; p 16 sobriety checkpoint, Getty Images; p 17 man taking breathalyzer test, Getty Images; p 19 shoplifter, Getty Images; p 21 man holding drug testing kit, AP Images; p 23 police officer making traffic stop, iStockphoto; p 24 police officer frisking suspect, Corbis; p 27 police stop man to search backpack, Corbis; p 29 police officer checking backpacks, Corbis; p 32 Supreme Court, iStockphoto.

Library of Congress Cataloging-in-Publication Data

Smith, Rich, 1954-
  Fourth Amendment : the right to privacy / Rich Smith.
    p. cm. -- (The Bill of Rights)
  Includes index.
  ISBN 978-1-59928-916-8
  1. Searches and seizures--United States--Juvenile literature. 2. Privacy, Right of--United States--Juvenile literature. 3. United States. Constitution. 4th Amendment--Juvenile literature. I. Title.

KF9630.Z9S65 2008
342.7308'58--dc22

2007014574

CONTENTS

INTRODUCTION

Many people warned T.L.O. (only her initials are used to protect her privacy) that she shouldn't smoke. But by age 14, she was hooked on cigarettes. Needing to light up often, she sometimes went to the girls' restroom at her New Jersey high school to have a few quick puffs between classes.

She got caught one day and was sent to the vice principal's office. His name was Theodore Choplick. Mr. Choplick ordered T.L.O. to open her purse. When she did, the vice principal could see a pack of cigarettes inside, plus something else: rolling papers, the kind used for preparing marijuana joints.

Mr. Choplick's eyebrow arched. He took the purse away from T.L.O. and started going through it. He found a sandwich bag filled with marijuana, a thick wad of cash, and a long list of names of classmates who owed her money. Taken together, the items made it look like T.L.O. was dealing drugs. Mr. Choplick called the police.

T.L.O. found herself in serious trouble. She was eventually convicted in juvenile court. However, her mother decided to fight the verdict. In the appeal she filed in court, Mother O. claimed that the school had violated T.L.O.'s constitutional rights when Mr. Choplick searched the purse. The rights were those spelled out in the Fourth Amendment of the Bill of Rights.

The Fourth Amendment declares: "The right of the people to be secure in their persons, houses, papers, and effects, against unreasonable searches and seizures, shall not be violated, and no Warrants shall issue, but upon probable cause, supported by Oath or affirmation, and particularly describing the place to be searched, and the persons or things to be seized."

Facing page: A student's backpack is searched by a security guard at Curie High School, in Chicago, Illinois. Recent court battles have been fought over whether searches similar to this violate students' Fourth Amendment rights.

THE KNOCK IN THE MIDDLE OF THE NIGHT

The government has many powers. Two that cause the most worry are the powers of search and seizure. These are good powers if used for the right reasons. However, they are very bad if used unjustly, especially by a dictatorship.

Unjustly is how these powers were often used in the time before the United States was born. Back then, it was not unusual for people to be searched and seized for no reason other than being disliked by the government. You became disliked perhaps because you showed disrespect for some important person in the government by not bowing down or not taking off your hat when he or she passed by. Or possibly it was because you were someone who went around spouting dangerous ideas about people being born with certain unalienable rights, such as the right to life, liberty, and the pursuit of happiness. Whatever the reason, the government simply wanted to get rid of you. Throwing you in prison was a good way to do just that.

First, however, the government had to arrest you. This usually began with a loud, angry knock on the front door in the middle of the night. Then, a small army of soldiers or law enforcers would push their way inside the home. They would rough up the person and clamp iron chains on his hands and feet. They might even put a sack over his head before taking him away. If he asked why he was being arrested, they might answer by striking him hard in the lower part of his back or behind the bend of his legs with a club or rifle butt. The invaders would also tear apart his home in search of anything to prove that he needed to be locked away, or even put to death.

Thankfully, the Founding Fathers of the United States did not want law enforcers to behave this way in the new nation being formed. First they created the Constitution. The Constitution is a document that describes how the U.S. government is set up and operated. It also explains the job of the president, the lawmakers of Congress, and the people who work as judges.

At the end of the Constitution are 27 additional instructions for the government. These are called amendments. The first 10 make up what is known as the Bill of Rights. The Bill of Rights lists the special freedoms every human is born with and is able to enjoy in America. Also, the Bill of Rights tells the government that it cannot stop people from fully using and enjoying those freedoms unless the government has an extremely good reason for doing so. Included in the Bill of Rights is an amendment that places limits on government's power to search and seize: the Fourth Amendment.

Below: The Fourth Amendment protects Americans from unreasonable police searches and seizures.

RULES THAT MUST BE FOLLOWED

In the many years since the Fourth Amendment was adopted, rules have been established to carefully control when and how searches and seizures are conducted. Some people argue that these rules make it too difficult for police and other law enforcers to catch criminals and win courtroom convictions. Other people argue the exact opposite. But that's not the point of the rules. The real point is to safeguard your right to be free from unreasonable searches and seizures.

The president, Congress, and the courts have all worked very hard over many, many years to develop these rules. One of the most important rules deals with the use of warrants. Warrants are like permission slips given to law enforcers so that they can legally search a specific place for evidence of a crime. Warrants are issued by a judge. The police must first convince the judge that they have good reason to suspect the place they want to search contains stolen goods, illegal items, or crime-scene materials.

Even if the judge issues a warrant, the police have strict limits on what they can search. They are allowed to search only the place and items named on the warrant. The search begins with the police presenting the warrant to the person who lives or works at the address shown on it. If no one answers the knock on the door, the police will let themselves in and leave the warrant somewhere inside where it can be easily seen by the person who lives or works there.

Facing page: After serving a warrant, federal agents search a home in San Diego, California, in an effort to find an illegal immigrant who had been ordered deported by an immigrations court.

The police must follow these and a number of other rules very carefully while conducting the search. If they break the rules, the crime evidence they collect won't be usable in court during the trial of the person or persons they end up arresting. Unusable evidence is officially known as excluded evidence. The rule about this is called the *exclusionary rule*.

The exclusionary rule dates back to 1914, when the Supreme Court decided the case of *Weeks v. United States*. Before this case, it didn't matter how the police obtained evidence. All of it could be introduced in court.

The case of *Weeks v. United States* began when authorities suspected Missouri businessman Fremont Weeks of being a criminal. The only problem was they had nothing to prove it. The police decided to raid his office in Kansas City, Missouri. They hoped this "fishing expedition" might uncover some evidence they could use to build a case. The police did this without first getting a warrant.

After turning his office upside down, police discovered records showing that Weeks had been mailing lottery tickets. It happened to be a federal crime for people to do that. This made the police happy because now they had the evidence needed to put Weeks behind bars for a very long time. But it did not turn out that way. The courts threw out the evidence because it was obtained illegally. And without that evidence, the government's case against Weeks fell apart. The Supreme Court had the final word on this. The justices wrote that the Fourth Amendment means what it says, and no longer would unreasonable searches be allowed.

Facing page: Two agents from the Federal Bureau of Investigation (FBI) stand guard outside an apartment building during a drug raid in Los Angeles, California. There are very strict rules that law enforcement officers must follow so that the evidence they uncover is allowable in a court of law.

WHEN NO WARRANT IS NEEDED

There are some exceptions to the rule forbidding evidence gathered without a warrant. The Supreme Court decided in the years after the *Weeks* case that there are certain situations when a warrant is not needed. The reason for these exceptions is that the police would never be able to properly protect the public if in every instance they first had to go to a judge and ask for a warrant.

Most of the exceptions to the rule about warrants involve situations where the target of a search is in plain sight of the police. The Supreme Court set the stage for this with its decision in the 1967 case of *Katz v. United States*. In this case, the justices defined a search as a hunt for evidence. But the evidence being hunted must be something kept in a private area. Also, it must be something stored in such a way that visitors to the private area can't see it unless the person it belongs to brings it out and shows it off.

This led the justices to the idea that if evidence is *not* in a private area and *not* stored in such a way as to keep it hidden, then the hunt for it cannot possibly count as a search. And if it does not count as a search, then police do not need a warrant to conduct it.

Here is an example of how that works: Police without a warrant can poke around in your trash cans at the curb in front of your house because those are in a public place where you can't really expect to hide what's in them. The same is true for things in your possession at the beach, in an airport, or even on farmland.

Facing page: Police officers generally do not need a warrant to make an arrest or gather evidence if a crime is happening in plain view.

Police have been legally able to look for evidence without a warrant on privately owned fields, pastures, and forests since 1984. That was the year the Supreme Court decided the case of *Oliver v. United States,* in which a Kentucky farmer by the name of Mr. Oliver had been arrested for growing marijuana. Police found his marijuana patch by entering through a gate and walking one mile (1.6 km) onto his property. In his criminal trial, Oliver tried to have the evidence against him thrown out. The police, he said, ignored his no-trespassing signs and came onto his land without a warrant. The court did not agree that the police acted illegally. Oliver appealed all the way to the Supreme Court. The justices sided with the lower courts and told Oliver that privacy was not possible on open land such as his. Since there was no privacy, there was no need for a warrant.

The Supreme Court later realized it went a little too far in the wrong direction with the rule about open lands. So an exception was created. This exception gives Fourth Amendment protection to the outdoor spaces directly alongside a home. The formal word for such spaces is *curtilage*, which can include a home's patio, enclosed garden, or fenced backyard. These are all areas in which most people would expect to have privacy. However, there are even exceptions to this exception. For instance, curtilage stops being a private area if it is viewed from high above, such as from a police helicopter.

Facing page: An Indiana State Police officer communicates with a helicopter hovering overhead during a drug raid near Wakefield, Indiana. Marijuana growers found the remote, washboard hills of southern Indiana perfect for production of the plant. Law enforcement officers generally don't need a warrant to search privately owned fields, pastures, or forests. Even in curtilage areas directly alongside homes, which are usually protected by the Fourth Amendment, police can search without a warrant if they observe criminal activity from plain view, even high above, such as from a helicopter.

LIMITING A RIGHT FOR THE GREATER GOOD

THE FOURTH AMENDMENT requires that Americans be free of unreasonable police searches and seizures. So why are sobriety checkpoints legal?

You've perhaps heard of sobriety checkpoints, or seen them. Maybe you've even been in a car that has passed through one. Sobriety checkpoints are roadblocks that law enforcers set up to catch drunk drivers. Police or state troopers put these checkpoints on the busiest streets, usually late at night or on weekends when they know the most number of drunks will be driving around. Typically, every car that enters the checkpoint is briefly stopped so that an officer can search for signs that the driver has been consuming alcohol. Anyone believed to be drunk is ordered to drive into an area off to the side of the road where other officers are waiting to conduct sobriety tests. Drivers who fail the tests are arrested and booked on the spot. In states where roadblocks are allowed, they are used also for checking to see if drivers and passengers are wearing seatbelts, and if infants are riding in approved car seats.

Below: A police officer checks a driver's license at a sobriety checkpoint in San Francisco, California, during a holiday-season campaign to reduce drunken driving.

Many civil liberties supporters are bothered by sobriety checkpoints because they involve searches without warrants and without probable cause. One who voiced his opposition was a man by the name of Rick Katz. In 1986, he sued to prevent the Michigan State Police Department from setting up sobriety checkpoints. The trial court judge ruled in favor of Katz and said that the roadblocks were a violation of the Fourth Amendment.

But the U.S. Supreme Court disagreed. The justices found that government's responsibility to ensure public safety by getting drunk drivers off the streets comes ahead of the people's right to be free from unreasonable search and seizure. This is what allows the government to briefly deny Americans one of their most basic rights whenever they drive through a sobriety checkpoint.

However, many defenders of civil liberties argue that sobriety checkpoints don't work. They say that most drunk drivers avoid them simply by turning onto a different street when they see them in the distance. Enough people are unhappy about sobriety checkpoints that 11 states have made it against the law for police to use them.

Above: A police officer administers a breathalyzer test to a man at a sobriety checkpoint in San Francisco, California.

We the People

Stopped Before the Evidence Disappears

There are other situations where no warrant is needed to conduct a police search. One of them is when law enforcers fear that a suspect might try to destroy evidence before they can obtain a judge's permission to search.

Another situation is when the police witness what appears to be a crime in the very act of being committed. For example: A police officer sees a man standing on a street corner in a rough neighborhood where illegal drugs are often sold. While the officer watches from a distance, the man is approached by a woman, who gives the man a wad of money. The man reaches into his pocket and hands her a plastic bag filled with white powder, which might be cocaine. The police officer, suspecting a crime is being committed, rushes over. The suspect sees the officer coming and runs away, disappearing into his home down the street. The officer follows the suspect into the house and handcuffs him, then searches the suspect's pockets and the house for evidence of drug dealing. The officer hits the jackpot when he opens a dresser drawer and looks inside, discovering weight scales, rolls of money, and bags of cocaine. All of this evidence is usually permissible in court, even though a warrant was not first obtained by the officer.

Warrants also are unnecessary if the search takes place in a government office, or in a prison cell. And there is no need for a warrant when the target of the search freely gives permission for authorities to have a look around.

It is important to understand that Fourth Amendment rules about search warrants apply only to police and other law enforcers under the control of federal, state, or local governments. The rules do not apply at all to searches conducted by private companies. For example, if a big corporation believes some of its employees are using company computers to run an Internet scam, the company can legally search for evidence by reading the workers' emails and data logs. The company can conduct this search in total secrecy if it wants.

A second example is if someone goes into a department store and is stopped by security guards on suspicion of shoplifting. No warrant is needed for the guards to search for stolen merchandise in the suspect's bags or underneath outer clothing.

Below: Private security guards do not need a search warrant to stop someone they suspect of shoplifting.

LESS PRIVACY AT SCHOOL

DO YOU PLAY football, basketball, baseball, or some other sport at your school? If so, then you probably were required to submit to drug testing before you could join the team. And then perhaps you were retested at random later in the season. You might not have thought it was such a big deal.

That can't be said of James Acton or his parents. They thought random drug testing was a very big deal. It upset them so much that they sued to stop their school district from demanding drug tests for student athletes. They felt that the tests violated the right of students to be free from unreasonable searches as guaranteed by the Fourth Amendment.

This all happened in the mid-1980s in Vernonia, Oregon. James was in the seventh grade at the time, and he wanted to try out for his school's football squad. But the school had made it a rule that anyone wanting to be on a team first had to be tested for drugs. Anyone who refused to take the test could not play. The school started this rule because drug abuse among the students was growing worse and worse. School officials discovered that the students abusing drugs the most were the athletes.

It made good sense to target athletes for drug testing. School officials believed that the players would be frightened by what testing might find. They believed this fear would cause the athletes to stop abusing drugs. They also believed that students who looked up to the athletes might also quit taking drugs.

The Supreme Court ruled on this case in 1995. It was known as *Vernonia School District 47J v. Acton*. The Court sided with the school district. The Court ruled that drug testing is reasonable under the Fourth Amendment because public school students cannot expect to have the same kind of privacy they enjoy at home. And besides, student athletes have always been required to submit to medical exams to make sure they are healthy enough to participate in sports. The Supreme Court justices decided that drug testing is the same kind of thing.

Facing page: An official with Drug Screen Compliance holds out a drug-testing kit similar to the kind used in many high school extracurricular drug-testing programs.

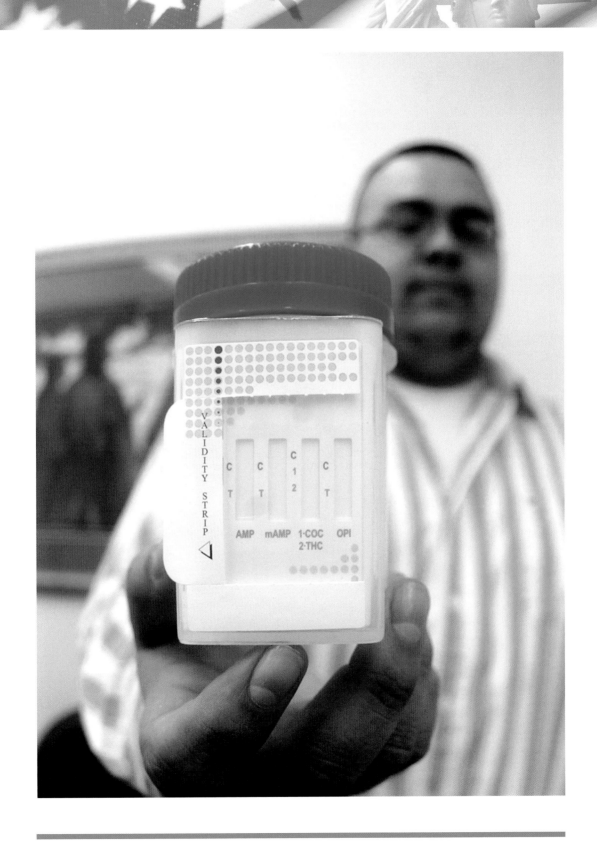

REASONABLE AND UNREASONABLE SEIZURE

Up to this point, we've looked at the Fourth Amendment's protections against unreasonable searches. Now let's look at its safeguards against unreasonable seizures. Seizure is what happens when law enforcers take something of yours to use as evidence in a crime case. Seizure is also what happens when law enforcers arrest you.

If you are temporarily prevented by police from freely going about your business, that too is considered a seizure under the Fourth Amendment. An example of this type of seizure is when you are driving a car and a traffic patrolman pulls you over to the side of the road to give you a ticket for speeding. You have not been arrested, but the patrolman has used his authority to detain you for the time it takes him to check your driver's license and car registration and write the ticket. Likewise, you have been seized but not been arrested if a police officer handcuffs you and places you in the back seat of his squad car. You are merely detained. You would only be arrested if the officer announced to you that he was in fact placing you under arrest.

You are not considered to have been seized at all if a law enforcer walks up to you in public and asks your permission to be questioned. In that situation, you would be free to ignore the officer's questions and walk away from him.

Facing page: A routine traffic stop is an example of a reasonable seizure. Police officers can use their authority to make you stop, check your identity, and issue you a ticket without formally arresting you.

Above: A bicycle patrol officer makes a Terry stop, frisking a suspect for possible weapons.

When you are seized by authorities, they are allowed in certain situations to conduct a type of search known as a frisk, or pat-down. This usually happens after the police have stopped you on the street for questioning because you're acting suspiciously, or simply because you are in a place where certain types of crime happen a lot. However, they can only frisk you if it looks like you are hiding a weapon under your clothes. The evidence for this would be, for instance, a bulge in your back pocket. The bulge might only be your wallet or an iPod, but the police don't like to take chances. The courts have said it is not unreasonable for them to protect their safety and the safety of others with the use of a pat-down search. This type of seizure has an official name. It is called a Terry stop. The name comes from the important 1968 Supreme Court case of *Terry v. Ohio*.

John W. Terry and a friend had been hanging out in front of a Cleveland, Ohio, store. A police detective saw them. The way the two were eyeing the store made the detective think they were planning to rob it. The detective walked up to Terry and his friend. He asked them what they were doing. Their answers only made the detective more certain a robbery was in the works. That's when he decided to frisk them. The pat-down turned up a gun hidden on each of them. The detective arrested them both for carrying concealed weapons.

At his trial, Terry tried to claim the search was a violation of the Fourth Amendment because he had not done anything illegal to justify such an invasion of his privacy. The court disagreed and sentenced Terry to three years in prison. Terry appealed his conviction. The case went to the Supreme Court, which agreed with the lower courts that the detective acted properly.

The rules about Terry stops have been refined and improved over the years. Basically, a Terry stop today cannot be conducted for longer than about 10 minutes if it is obvious that you have neither committed a crime nor are planning one. Also, the questions that police ask can only be about whatever it is they stopped you for. For example, if they stop you because they suspect you might be selling drugs, they are not allowed to also ask if you had anything to do with a recent bank holdup.

The Name Game

NEARLY HALF THE STATES have laws that require persons detained by the police to tell what their name is when asked. These are known as stop-and-identify laws, and they are fully constitutional. In a 2004 ruling, the Supreme Court said that it is not an unreasonable violation of the Fourth Amendment for law enforcers to demand the name of anyone they question during a Terry stop.

A Terry stop is when police briefly seize someone they notice acting suspiciously or who happens to be in the wrong place at the wrong time. During a Terry stop, police are allowed to briefly question the person they have seized in order to learn whether he or she can be considered a crime suspect.

Until the Supreme Court's ruling, a person detained in a Terry stop did not have to answer any of the questions asked by the police. That included questions about his or her name. That changed with the Court's decision in the case of *Hiibel v. Sixth Judicial District Court of Nevada*. From then on, a detained person could still refuse to answer police questions during the stop, but was required to at least reveal his or her identity.

This all got started in May 2000 when a Winnemucca, Nevada, deputy sheriff was sent to check on a report of an angry man and woman screaming at one another by the side of a road. The argument had ended by the time the deputy arrived. He found a woman sitting in a pickup truck and a man standing next to it. He approached the man and asked his name. The man refused to answer the question. Suspecting that the man had been driving while intoxicated, the deputy asked him his name 10 more times. Finally, he arrested the man for obstructing a crime investigation.

The obstruction charge was made because the man would not tell his name. But not telling his name was also a violation of Nevada's stop-and-identify law. Eventually, the authorities determined that the man's name was Larry Dudley Hiibel. He was convicted in court, and then appealed the verdict on the grounds that the stop-and-identify law amounted to an unreasonable search and seizure. Hiibel lost all the way to the Supreme Court.

Above: An officer stops a man to inspect his backpack before entering New York's Grand Central Station. People who are stopped by police are required to identify themselves.

THE BIG PICTURE

The mother of New Jersey high school student T.L.O. (who we talked about at the beginning of this book) thought that the seizure of her cigarette-smoking daughter and the search of the drug-filled purse were both unreasonable acts under the Fourth Amendment. That is why she appealed her daughter's conviction. After listening to the arguments, the New Jersey Supreme Court decided that T.L.O.'s Fourth Amendment rights had indeed been violated by Vice Principal Choplick. But the story did not end there.

The school district appealed to the U.S. Supreme Court, and in 1985 the High Court overturned the New Jersey court's decision. The U.S. Supreme Court held that Mr. Choplick's search of T.L.O.'s purse was perfectly legal, for several different reasons. One, a school official has the right to search a student's belongings if that's what it takes to prevent school rules from being broken. Two, a school official has the right to search a student's belongings if the official has good reason to believe the student has committed a crime. Three, students voluntarily give up most of their rights to keep possessions private when they bring them onto public school property. Four, plainly visible evidence of a crime gives school officials the authority to conduct a thorough search for more evidence and for actual illegal items or stolen goods.

The painful lesson T.L.O. learned from this was not that smoking and drug abuse are dangerous habits that lead to big trouble (they are, and they do). The lesson she really learned was that her right to be free from unreasonable searches and seizures is not an absolute right. In truth, it is a limited right. It has to be. If it was not a limited right, it would be impossible for government to carry out its main duty of keeping the public safe and the streets peaceful.

One of the jobs of the court system in the United States is to find a proper balance between the rights of individuals and the responsibilities of government. Sometimes the courts favor one too much over the other. But that is okay. Sooner or later, a proper balance is reached. That is the beauty of the American Constitution and its Bill of Rights. These important documents provide a framework for liberty that never stops being able to satisfy the needs of the people.

Below: Students have their bags and backpacks checked by a law enforcement officer before entering a high school in Dallas, Texas.

GLOSSARY

Amendment

When it was created, the Constitution wasn't perfect. The Founding Fathers wisely added a special section. It allowed the Constitution to be changed by future generations. This makes the Constitution flexible. It is able to bend to the will of the people it governs. Changes to the Constitution are called amendments. The first 10 amendments are called the Bill of Rights. An amendment must be approved by two-thirds of both houses of Congress. Once that happens, the amendment must be approved by three-fourths of the states. Then it becomes law. This is a very difficult thing to do. The framers of the Constitution didn't want it changed unless there was a good reason. There have been over 9,000 amendments proposed. Only 27 of them have been ratified, or made into law. Some amendments changed the way our government works. The Twelfth Amendment changed the way we elect our president. The Twenty-Second Amendment limits a president to two terms in office. Constitutional amendments have also increased the freedoms of our citizens. The Thirteenth Amendment finally got rid of slavery. And the Nineteenth Amendment gave women the right to vote.

Curtilage

Outdoor space that is directly alongside a home, such as a patio or fenced backyard. Curtilage is normally granted Fourth Amendment protection against searches without a warrant, although there are some exceptions.

Dictatorship

A country with a single leader who rules with total power. Citizens of a dictatorship have little or no say in how their country is run. Dictators usually gain their position, and keep their powers, through the use of military force. The Constitution was written to avoid dictatorships. It splits government into three distinct parts: the presidency, Congress, and the Supreme Court. This separation of power keeps any one individual from becoming a dictator.

Exclusionary Rule

Rules and laws that determine whether evidence gathered by law enforcement personnel is allowable in a court of law.

Founding Fathers

The men who participated in the Constitutional Convention in 1787, especially the ones who signed the Constitution. Some of the Founding Fathers included George Washington, Benjamin Franklin, John Rutledge, Gouverneur Morris, Alexander Hamilton, and James Madison.

High Court

Another name for the United States Supreme Court.

Lawsuit

A legal way to settle a dispute in which both sides argue their case in front of a judge or jury in a court of law. The person who has been wronged is called the plaintiff. The person being sued is called the defendant. Plaintiffs and defendants can be individuals, or they can be businesses or government entities, such as corporations or towns. People can even sue the United States, which is how many cases are filed involving the Constitution and violation of rights.

Ratification

The process of making a proposed law or treaty officially valid. Constitutional amendments are ratified when they are approved by two-thirds of both houses of Congress, and by three-fourths of the states.

Sue

To bring a lawsuit against a person or institution in a court of law.

Supreme Court

The United States Supreme Court is the highest court in the country. There are nine judges on the Supreme Court. They make sure local, state, and federal governments are following the rules spelled out in the United States Constitution. Our understanding of the Constitution evolves over time. It is up to the Supreme Court to decide how the Constitution is applied to today's society. When the Supreme Court rules on a case, other courts in the country must follow the decision in similar situations. In this way, the laws of the Constitution are applied equally to all Americans.

INDEX

A

Acton, James 20

B

Bill of Rights 4,
7, 28

C

Choplick,
Theodore 4, 28
Cleveland, OH 25
Congress, U.S. 7,
8
Constitution, U.S.
7, 28
curtilage 14

E

exclusionary rule
11

F

Founding Fathers
7
Fourth
Amendment 4,
8, 11, 14, 16, 17,
19, 20, 22, 25,
26, 28

H

Hiibel, Larry
Dudley 26
*Hiibel v. Sixth
Judicial District
Court of Nevada*
26

K

Kansas City, MO
11
Katz, Rick 17
*Katz v. United
States* 12
Kentucky 14

M

Michigan
State Police
Department 17
Missouri 11

N

Nevada 26
New Jersey 4, 28
New Jersey
Supreme Court
28

O

Oliver 14
*Oliver v. United
States* 14

S

stop-and-identify
laws 26
Supreme Court
U.S. 11, 12, 14,
17, 20, 25, 26,
28

T

Terry, John W. 25
Terry stop 25, 26
Terry v. Ohio 25

U

United States 6, 28

Above: The
United States
Supreme Court in
Washington, D.C.

V

Vernonia, OR 20
*Vernonia School
District 47J v.
Acton* 20

W

Weeks, Fremont
11
*Weeks v. United
States* 11, 12
Winnemucca, NV
26